STORIES TOO FIERY TO SING
TOO WATERY TO WHISPER

other books by the author

POETRY
Dawn Visions
Burnt Heart/Ode to the War Dead
This Body of Black Light Gone Through the Diamond
The Desert is the Only Way Out
The Chronicles of Akhira
The Blind Beekeeper
Mars & Beyond
Laughing Buddha Weeping Sufi
Salt Prayers
Ramadan Sonnets
Psalms for the Brokenhearted
I Imagine a Lion
Coattails of the Saint
Abdallah Jones and the Disappearing-Dust Caper (illustrated by the author)
Love is a Letter Burning in a High Wind
The Flame of Transformation Turns to Light
Underwater Galaxies
The Music Space
Cooked Oranges
Through Rose Colored Glasses
Like When You Wave at a Train and the Train Hoots Back at You
In the Realm of Neither
The Fire Eater's Lunchbreak
Millennial Prognostications
You Open a Door and it's a Starry Night
Where Death Goes
Shaking the Quicksilver Pool
The Perfect Orchestra
Sparrow on the Prophet's Tomb
A Maddening Disregard for the Passage of Time
Stretched Out on Amethysts
Invention of the Wheel
Sparks Off the Main Strike
Chants for the Beauty Feast
In Constant Incandescence
Holiday from the Perfect Crime
The Caged Bear Spies the Angel
The Puzzle
Ramadan is Burnished Sunlight
Ala-udeen & The Magic Lamp (illustrated by the author)
The Crown of Creation (illustrated by the author)
Blood Songs
Down at the Deep End (with drawings by the author)
Next Life
A Hundred Little 3D Pictures
He Comes Running (chapbook)
Miracle Songs for the Millennium
The Throne Perpendicular to All that is Horizontal
The Soul's Home
Some
Facing Mecca
Eternity Shimmers Time Holds its Breath
Stories Too Fiery to Sing Too Watery to Whisper

THEATER / THE FLOATING LOTUS MAGIC OPERA COMPANY
The Walls Are Running Blood
Bliss Apocalypse

STORIES TOO FIERY TO SING
TOO WATERY TO WHISPER

•

DANIEL ABDAL-HAYY MOORE

June 13 — October 24, 2005

Preface by Tom Clark

The Ecstatic Exchange
2014
Philadelphia

Stories Too Fiery to Sing Too Watery to Whisper
Copyright © 2014 Daniel Abdal-Hayy Moore
All rights reserved.
Printed in the United States of America

For quotes any longer than those for critical articles and reviews, contact:
The Ecstatic Exchange,
6470 Morris Park Road, Philadelphia, PA 19151-2403
email: abdalhayy@danielmoorepoetry.com

First Edition
ISBN: 978-0-578-15008-6 (paper)
Published by *The Ecstatic Exchange*,
6470 Morris Park Road, Philadelphia, PA 19151-2403

Cover art by the author
Back cover photograph by Malika Moore
Bee by author

DEDICATION

To
Shaykh ibn al-Habib
(and the continuation of the Habibiyya)
Shaykh Bawa Muhaiyuddeen,
all shuyukh of instruction and ma'arifa
Baji Tayyaba Khanum
of the unsounded depths

*The earth is not bereft
of Light*

CONTENTS

Words for a Preface by Tom Clark   8
The Delirious Archer   11
The Star Catcher   12
The Dead Pirate's One Last Swing   14
The Secret of Poetry   16
Words and Birdsong   19
Zero   21
Dream-Words upon Waking   23
Lost Identity   24
Harbingers of Death   27
Amethyst Thimble   30
Travel Notes   32
Orangutan or Pit   36
The High Potency of Certain Moments   38
Somewhere in the Remote Arctic   39
British Air Flight 68 to Heathrow   40
Perfect World   41
Afloat Behind the Face of Things   42
The Hearts of the Holiest   44
The Dying Room   46
The Cure   49
The Old Cracked Bell   51
A Little Course in Miracles   53
A Short Treatise on Nightmares   55
Dogs Bark in Montefrio   57
The Old Ones and the Young Ones   59
The Ski Slope Inevitable   61
Look at the Door   63
Spat Sunflower Seed Shells   66
The Lace of Light   68

Continuous Travel   71
The Illumination of Fray Luis De Salamanca de Crisis y Bendición   73
Inventory   78
Smudges   80
Thirteen Peacocks   81
Saintly Places   83
The Bell Unrung   85
Scratching Sound   86
The Silver Boat   91
Death With a Green Umbrella / An Entertainment   92
Albino Silver Fox   95
The Red Fez   97
Pruning   100
One Totally Tall Tale   102
The Seven Dwarves   104
All From a Dot   105
The Imam of Our Mosque   107
My Usual Airplane Apprehensions   110
While Waiting to Appear in Traffic Court   112
Conversing Beyond the End of Time   113
The Ballad of the Tyrant   115
The Usual Clocks Ticking   117
Dear Eyes   119
It's True   121
"Spare Parts Spare Parts!"   124
Conversations Over the Graveyard   126
The Last Poem   129
The Brother to the Dog   131
The Fire Broke Out   132

INDEX   136

WORDS FOR A PREFACE

by Tom Clark

The pleasure of feeling the poem discovering itself is always a particular joy in reading this poet — especially so because the voyage of discovery each poem seems to make is, finally, a journey toward the light — whether inside or outside, grand and glorious or fine and concentrated and elusive and just or almost entirely out of reach... yet somehow still in there or out there somewhere, waiting to be found.

And yes, we're all included in that trip the poem offers, and there is no charge, and no baggage required. Indeed, we learn to understand that there is no baggage we will need on that trip, the baggage would only be an impediment in any case.

What I respect most in the work is the humility and respect that acknowledges the collective of all souls and refuses to escape into the unfortunately now all too common mode of not saying whatever it is the poem wants to say... because of course that boils down in most cases either to nothing at all, or something too banal and/or trivial to make plain without embarrassment. So that the cover stories, the inertia and evasion along with the coy and clever construction of coded hints and vaguely connected clue-bits woven into the precious fabric of a reiterative whinging private narrative become a substitute for the poem that isn't there.

With Abdal-Hayy I never feel that, and am instead relieved to feel that I can actually get what the poem is getting at, and that it is something that matters, some matter of small or large joy of delight or suffering or knowledge or vision, in which we all may share, and from which we all may learn, illuminating, humbling, uplifting all at once, as it seems poetry was once meant to be, before it became the embarrassing competitive business it is today — something hardly worth speaking of, especially when in the presence of the real article.

In the Koran, one verse is for the sake of the state of the believers. After that, He says a verse for the sake of the state of the unbelievers. However, in the world of love, all is gentleness. There is no severity. It's quite some time now that I have come out of severity. But, right here, severity is near. Hell is on this side. When you pass beyond hell, paradise is on the other side of the Narrow Path. The world of gentleness is without end and without shore.
— Shams-i Tabrizi
(Me & Rumi, #79, translated by William C. Chittick)

THE DELIRIOUS ARCHER

This is the story of the delirious archer
who could shoot in a state no one would say
was sober yet he hit the bullseye every time

He split eyelashes saplings feathers floating in air in absolute
half yet was so deliriously ecstatic as the world
showed itself to him fully jeweled in every aspect
kaleidoscopically singing in close harmony and revealing to his
bedazzled eyes
the secret meanings of things entirely that he

couldn't be given seemingly normal responsibilities
but was for all intents and purposes to everyone else
a complete idiot always smiling when not laughing and
always laughing when not sobbing

6/13

THE STAR CATCHER

There was a woman of slim stature and bony structure
who claimed to have caught the essence of a star in a
dish

It did glow there on its own and spread a
strong yellow-white light in the room so bright
you had to shield your eyes when you entered there

She kept the secret to herself as she showed visitors the
consequence of her remarkable feat

The giant growth of normally tiny flowers such as
forget-me-nots which from now on from their size
should forevermore be called "forget-me-nevers"

The odd iridescence shimmering from all the
walls and ceilings of all the rooms in her house

and most wondrous of all a totally transparent
ceiling to the room the dish sits in so that you can now
see into the deepest areas of space with perfect
ease and marvel at the abundance of completely functioning
galaxies and solar systems like bubbles on an infinite black lake
happily twinkling and spinning in their own evanescent orbits
suspended in a seeming endlessness of nothingness

And she stands with her hands at her sides
with her face turned up and the great pale oval shells of her

eyelids closed and a smile on her face as unforgettable as her
flowers as we backed out of her house amazed to the sound of

piping symphonic flute music as of distant high-pitched

but very fragile tinkling of glass in a slow wind

                                                                6/13

THE DEAD PIRATE'S ONE LAST SWING

He was really a heap of rotted clothing mostly
black wool and badly sewn patches with
hemp

It's not that he had a peg-leg or hook for hand or
one eye the other red and bulbous under a patch
so much as that he had all these things
plus a parrot

Yet he was the kindest person you'd ever hope to meet always
sharing his one biscuit with birds and
fondly brushing a mongrel actually more flea-bitten and
worse off than he

The fact that he played Chopin and Schubert with
effervescent finesse finer than any concert pianist alive
might but shouldn't come as a surprise brought up
as he was by missionaries in the West Indies

But the fact that at night he wept over this
foul world so much that he left his body and

rose above it in a yellow cloud to roam from
room to room wherever people might suffer any fraction of
infraction infarction or pain
and touch them on their eyes hands or legs where his own
phantom limbs and orbs had been with no trace of

envy though really being a disabled pirate with an
angelic rather than demonic heart might be a
bit hard to swallow but after all

aren't we all?

                                                    6/14

THE SECRET OF POETRY

One line lands in a word and one word
lands in a line and
there you have it the secret of poetry

A steep incline guarded by panthers

A dense forest where lit periwinkles and dizzy
fairies jostle for space between leaves and flowers
each yelling inaudibly that they are the
guardians of poetry

A sudden drop out of nowhere into a sudden drop into nowhere
guarded by lines of army ants and one nearly eaten
brigadier who used to be in uniform though now his
real bony armaments show through

Or it's a long stretch with few houses and some
snoozing beasts and you can barely see the
mountains for the haze and the heat itself is
unbearable

Now getting on your hands and knees about poetry is
definitely preferable to sitting in a comfy armchair
and getting face down in total prostration is
certainly preferable to hands and knees and from there
a secret meeting in a dark marketplace by The Jeweler's stall
on a Thursday night with enough currency to carry away
something of inestimable value

guarded by two giant mastiffs in spike collars who
haven't eaten for weeks

Lift the little cut turquoises and put them into place next to the
evenly-placed sliver abalone chips in such a pattern and at
such an angle that they'll catch the light fully before it
fades to zero

And better than full prostration
there is actually nothing at all

Let everything slide out fingers and toes
and when you later settle into bed let your
extremities unflex the world entirely so your body's
little electric nerve serpents can wiggle out and be
gone though they served their purpose well

Poetry that doesn't adorn the corridors of heaven
and the doors of Paradise covered with signs
is worth nothing more than paper foil cut into shapes
and easily crinkled into small balls and tossed
over forgotten fences

People spend so much time saying nothing worth saying and
hearing nothing worth remembering as the big clock
moves forward on giant claw feet and the

geese try again this year to find their
own way home

guarded by poets in flammable garments

lounging outside the fireworks factory

hoping midnight will still find them

in one piece there

when the dawn comes

                                                                                 6/15

WORDS AND BIRDSONG

I'm saddened by the fact that I can't
adequately describe the sound of those birds
out in the dark of the undarkening dawn
whose song carries on as I write this

and the effect their whistly upturned melodies
have on me in my room just inside from where
they're singing

One song just a slide up-scale tweeting
another up-and-down notes varied sliding
poignant beyond words another just little
note-bursts short and sweeter than sweet

Yet later these words will seem flat
though now while the birds are singing they kind of
represent their singing inadequately but
attempting to be something worthy even though

what words are and sound like aren't what
birdsong is and sounds like for their

grammar is repetitive and insistent in ways
words may not need to be

plus they're up in trees or sailing in the air while
singing though generally I think they sing when situated on a
branch or twig or treetop rather than

whistling on the wing

Words are so wordy in comparison

I wonder if the response to them is the same?

Why birds sing?

For themselves?

For that inexplicable thing that

endless solitary glorying?

6/15

ZERO

Finally the very venerable Ancient of Days and
Afternoons who was of a vaguely cactus shape

told how he'd realized one evening perhaps full moon
that to reach God he'd have to become less and less
not more and more

So he dropped his pomposity which thudded on the
earth like a bass drum and began carrying himself
less like Mussolini or a bantam rooster
and more like an open space where new things might
enter (and not feel afraid) and settle in for good

And then he lopped off the branches of his
various pretensions and at that point even his
shadow grew thinner since it didn't have to
do the work of three or four all seeming to be
one thing or another they weren't

And instead he cultivated the opposite of an
identity for himself he adopted a
kind of anonymity and a glow began in his
heart cavity that gradually grew bigger

And he thinned himself out in various ways and
lowered himself down sometimes painfully
lower and lower even sometimes below earth-level
and in becoming less and less instead of more and

more he began to see the Greater Entity the
Glorious Gardener and Compassionate Executioner Who
both lops and reprieves at the same instant

and so releases what never in the first place
had any intrinsic reality
from its basic false assumption that he

exist at all

so that the indefinable reality Reality itself more and more

might (and did) take first place in that

person who through becoming less and less
more and more began to resemble

zero

                                                                  6/21

DREAM-WORDS UPON WAKING

Hold on to what I have given you

It is not righteousness in itself

You have to make it yours

                                                        6/25

LOST IDENTITY

1

The story of a lost identity
lost upon winning and won upon losing circularity
in chase mode round and round

like Michaelangelo's slack skin on the Sistine
eyeholes and mouth but skull gone all hanging slack
and slithery as pizza dough
so our identities go and keep on going and
leave us yet something like a
spark that can rekindle the all remains and goes on
past the black velvet drapery that is

mirror on one side and singing constellations on the
other that is ourselves as we were before
the first tree found us and made us one of its
branches in this world

Naked dancing might be forbidden but not naked
being which is what we all are
when our story begins

2

Hololotop on top of the world

raises his hands and the sun entangles there

Lowers his head and the moon shines

He has no special powers

Standing kneedeep letting the river waters flow

forward between his legs all agurgle

He seems to stand still but is moving

as fast as the river waters move

as he well knows

if he but knew

3

Dissolving is hardly an alternative
to solidity when one is satisfactorily solid
and used to it all these years from

the first liquid drop boring its
way into the world's eggy nucleus

clothing our bones with flesh to walk abroad

with boater hats and strong stride down

wide avenues to night's encroaching tide

4

Out the airplane window the sky is suddenly white
like an angel's backside or perhaps just one
tiny feather-blade from its too enormous wing to be
comprehended now covering us as we

tilt forward to our earthly destination

That one solid feather blade covering the
airplane window with its slow flash of nearly
blinding light

I'm not yet ready to dissolve away on a
sigh or even high note unless His fated

beckoning overpower me and the

blinding white light of His angels' blade
take me over

entirely

7/1

HARBINGERS OF DEATH

Imagine for a moment that it's not The
Angel of Death who comes as harbinger of death
but instead say

The Frog of Death who hops in one day with
poppy eyes and turned-down mouth and maybe

zaps a fly with long red tongue unblinking just to
underline the fact that we're soon to also be

zapped by a living carnivorous something that will
consume us into its greater presence or

in this case (by one perspective) absence

Or it could be The Tiny Pony of Death one of those
pastel ones with a little silver saddle tied on by

ribbon and of course it's empty so the little horse
paws the ground a few times tap tap with its

little right hoof to show its mild impatience and
we look down by the open door it came in by

and without looking up at us it taps the ground one more
time like a clock striking twelve and there's that

empty silver saddle gleaming in the fading light

Or The Moth of Death that lands on our forefinger as we're
gesturing in animated conversation about some

surprising news we've just heard some tidbit
gleaned from the airwaves and just

nonchalantly The Moth of Death appears and after a
few poignant and beautiful flutters lands on our

forefinger upraised as we make our point
only its point is made more pointedly and more poignantly

Ah all these little messengers instead of The
Angel of Death who may or may not appear in

physical form but we feel the instant chill
hear the gunning of God's engine just out-or-inside

our door

and know by our instinct from birth it's time for the
ultimate exit strategy to come into play

And we hope there's time for fond farewells and the
tidying up behind us so we aren't like a bad

party leaving empties and ashtrays overflowing and a
stale smell in the air of the various modes of

distraction we get up to to try to thwart and
obviate death's intersection at the confrontational crossroad

that suddenly and absolutely narrows our choices to none

And we can go singing celestial praises or wailing like walruses
talking in tongues or clutching the rug for dear life

eyes wide open in sagacious onlooker essence or
clamped shut insulted and betrayed by our

own unpreparedness

that frog or tiny pastel
horse or moth or shimmering shadow across a
bright lake or falling tree-bough in slow motion
straight down at us or just a

tiny pin dropping from a simple height that

clangs to the floor like a gong

7/5

AMETHYST THIMBLE

for Salihah on her birthday

An amethyst thimble with topaz inlay was
known in the kingdom to cause serious miracles
such as saving babies from crib death or from
various physical defects or a failure of faith when

whoever wears it thinks of an
emerald green hill with a trapezoidal crystal on it that reflects back
the full moon and casts a ray of its light onto the
exposed chin of the subject in need while the wearer sings a
spontaneous song and imagines a black panther prowling
the city in search of the trapezoidal crystal but whose
burning ruby eyes catch sight of a pure white
gazelle bathing under a turquoise waterfall and bending
down to drink suddenly sees itself and is

transformed back into the pristine Prince from a
noble family who was bewitched just after birth but who
continued to grow and is older now

standing in young adulthood naked in the
rainbow waterspray just as late afternoon hits between
zenith and sunset and a spider crawls up his
leg from a fern nearby and up to his midriff but he
doesn't swat it away instead he leans down and
greets it and speaks to it as to another person

and the spider drops and begins to spin a web from his
thigh to a small extended hickory branch and the
Prince stands very still until the spider is not only
done with a perfectly symmetrical web but after a
day lying in wait catches a white moth who
drunk on a nectar she'd just found flutters
haphazardly into it and so becomes the spider's lunch
who runs out on his tightrope and starts

spinning mummy wrap around her at which point she
looks at him through her tiny moth eyes and cries out
"You can't do this to me! I know your grandmother!"

And the spider laughs his vicious spidery laugh and asks her his
grandmother's name and the
moth sings out with unusual sweetness *"Her name's*

Spoldoranax" and at that
the spider staggers back on his string and looks at her with
sudden tenderness and

with his mandibles cuts away all the sticky miles of
winding-silk and sets her free

The miracle you wish for

takes place

the very moment you wish it

TRAVEL NOTES

1

A little pair of shoes and a hemp wristwatch
an extra pair of sox and a smear of Botticelli blue
a silver swipe across the cheek for luck and a
Brazilian bicycle for fast getaways to a
deep internal rhythm

These are the things to take for travel across this globe
if any insight's to be gained

including a signed paper and a sudden
change of heart up that hill or down that alleyway
at that bewitching time of day

"Every ward's full of transparent ghosts" you say
but *"no more full and no more transparent
than usual"* I say

and you nod sleepily as we continue on our way

2

Travel's always a ticklish affair
You leave your house and click the door
and face one of the outer or nearer planets

spreading your arms as if to fly

and nothing in front of you really but joy and
improvisation lumbering giant black elephants of
the Unforeseen already on parade in the invisible and
God's true Mercy falling already in a rain as fine as
silver powder in a steady and continuous stream

And unused tickets and strange forgotten ticket stubs in your
left jacket pocket because you haven't worn that
particular jacket since the last time you traveled
away from the Mother Ship

And the Faith Tester is already plugged in and
ticking like a taxi meter for the times there's no
bed or car or dinner or road where the map says the
road is supposed to be in little snaky red dashes

And free fall is the norm and reaching for the
umbilical is the norm and wishing your own
front step were the next step is the norm but the

next step is the uphill certain one required of someone who's
suddenly and floatingly free from this world

entirely enough to find the

key the stone the leaf the unfound door the sharp butcher knife the
rind of old cheese edible by moonlight

God's personal pocket mirror

a pair of planetary dice the throw of neither of which ever

abolishes chance

3

We arrive at our destination and there's a

tank of blue water suspended so
high in the sky we can't tell where
water ends and sky begins

A benign Face bending over all

And a house in a tree with ladder and chimney
smoking and songs from inside that correspond to

ships at sea in their wavering melodies of
forward slosh and sideward tilt preceded by
dolphins

A cuckoo clock deep inside tells the hour by
chirps and the pots and pans hanging on their
hooks resound like gamelans as the air inside moves aside

to let us inside

House turned inside out or outside in

Arrival turned inside out to become
starting point toward the olive groves of our
emancipation from matter altogether

over rolling hills in every direction

as bodiless as day is

7/12

ORANGUTAN OR PIT

Asked to choose between the flaming orangutan sitting
in the middle of his path or a

pit so deep and wide some are known to have
never come out

Onyx Blue Sky whose true name was
Turquoise Green Earth chose the pit and began his

nighttime exploration lampless and compassless

saying goodbye to all his mothers and fathers all the way
back to Father Adam and Lady Eve

and categorizing his lifetime of experiences for easy
reference into

Exalting Exasperating Expanding Expenditures and Exiting

Then with a graceful flourish he
lowered himself down with the words
"Remember the Kokomo! Remember Yoko Ono!
Remember in Esperanto or whatever tongue you wag but
wag it for God!" on his quivering lips

and just like that he was gone

We heard his yelling and glorious shouting get

fainter and then more echoey then deeper then
more like migrating birds then more like
plagues of locusts then dark locomotives then
distant locutions then whispers of fortune and
future misfortunes until we looked around at
each other and ourselves and saw we were

alone and soon to be faced with the same

dilemma

And some chose the orangutan

7/12

THE HIGH POTENCY OF CERTAIN MOMENTS

*"The high potency of certain moments doesn't
extinguish the low potency of certain others*

We're all heading toward the Apocalypse

*A cool head
a heart engaged in invocation"*

Then my pen sprouted wings and flew off to a
mountaintop where it fathered a brood of

similar egrets

7/13

SOMEWHERE IN THE REMOTE ARCTIC

Somewhere in the remote arctic there's a
vast sea of oval glaciers each set as if
in ivory and extending across the
expanse as if providing steppingstones for God

over black water

from the Inconceivable to the Incontrovertible
as He in an inscrutable mechanism proceeds on
His endless rounds throughout the

known and unknown universes indefatigably
assisting and peeling back and revealing the
core and manifesting it then concealing it back inside
its rippling golden sheath across each
edgeless horizon as if it were the sun but it is
not the sun it's a seed the size of the sun

inside our hearts

worshipping within its own solar heaven

and melting each manifestation back again
into its reflecting pool like amber honey

over which he bends His Face

7/14

BRITISH AIR FLIGHT 68 TO HEATHROW

All the babies in the world are crying
behind my seat on British Air flight 68 to Heathrow

All the old men in the world are reading their
scriptures as we prepare to take off

All the people in the world are in this airplane
as it pops into the air like the top off a
carbonated soda

All the destinations in the world pass below us
as we rise above the world on our way somewhere
in this world at a precise point on this world

while for a time aloft we may not be totally
of this world but become slightly akin
to angels and eagles in their ever-watchful flights
over this world

searching for lovers in their delirious solitudes
not of this world

but of the Hidden Creator of this world

manifest in the secret and self-evident
signs of this world

7/14

PERFECT WORLD

What a perfect world!
Where roosters crow up the sun

and furniture left too long gets
dust on it

the same dust we will become one day

of no use to anyone

7/16

AFLOAT BEHIND THE FACE OF THINGS

He had permission to only speak when spoken to
only look when looked at
only walk ahead when ahead walked him there
only stand in a standing he was given and he
was given good standing

Only participate when participation somehow
parted in such a way as to let him in

And in these straits and strictest circumstances
he saw what was seen and heard the
hearing in which even a pin dropping
was choirs

He was not left alone for long since what
came to him became him

His activity in this world became a phenomenon like
rain or the weather or a sweet drink in the
sun or an arc seen to connect two points
with no superfluous engineering but just enough to
go from point to point

essentialized accompanied by larks and
heavenly phrases as his eyes surveyed a world
of domelike stars become unlidded as seeing itself
poured into him from a great distance somewhere
beyond our single system

And his speech was never more than could
pound a nail or set free desperate
animals from their traps

And among humans he was that rarity
a silent witness and an ever-present cog when a
wheel needs turning or a soul dependent on the
wrong ledge needs anchoring to real landmass or
liberated from the ocean's lunar levels as a
daily round and set free into the deepest cosmic limitations

Here was a heart that knew no numbness

A pot of varied flowers spoke to him from the forest of the center

afloat behind the face of things

7/17

THE HEARTS OF THE HOLIEST

Bright as a million rosy stars as they
pan across our horizon on their little
metal disk and disappear

More silent than the sleep of fish in the
deepest pits of ocean depths in the darkest
dark where no sound ever was

And yet clearer than every arctic pool that
reflects more than sky and clouds as endless
cloudlessness but even
dimensions beyond our usual twelve or fourteen
with their absolutely sharp chromium flashes of
prismatic color and extensions into uncreated worlds more
alive even than ours has ever been or
ever will be

are the hearts of these godly ones who are not
hidden behind the mountains of our monotonous days
but even when they show their faces we might say
*"Another human face a bit shyer or sweeter than
the others"* but all God's bright silent and clear
attributes are working their giant turbine-driven engines in their
hearts and in so doing
are moving the entire universe itself through the stars
and depths and dimensions to His Throne Room

where a single whisper contains the speech of millennia of

thought and its flawed but perfect expression and a

single glance contains all the purest eye contact of
millennia of pupils dilating and contracting at the

sight of their beloveds and cherished loved ones

                                                            7/17

THE DYING ROOM

The living room is ten times smaller than the
dying room which monopolizes the South
Quadrant

though it's presided over by He Who Would Not Be
Named with a simple vocable or two

and whose aspect really is that of skylarks who
fly straight up into the air while singing then
dive again straight down

for this is the Dying Room

A suite of silvery furniture each designated for a
different phase including the replacement of the
self with its usual limitations with one seemingly
small and useless and ignored by all

but which sights distressed ships far off at sea and is
able to save them by a heartbeat that throws
cascades of light like an iron chain around their
sad distressed bulks

and lets God's countenance through the way a
dust-caked mirror cleaned with strong rubbing will seemingly
as if by magic let an image reflect in it that before
was just ambivalent smudge yet ambivalent smudge we
mistook for living

Other chambers in the dying room have
fountains of various colored waters and baths of
various mixtures of natural herbs and the incantations of
various saints into whose depths old depths

dissolve and new depths emerge as if
looking into a canyon and seeing sky or

into sky and seeing canyons all angel-thick with
recipes for almost instantaneous transformation from
semblance to reality and self-invention to
our essence from before the creation that casts aside darkness
the same as we know now but now with knowledge

reversed or turned inside-out to reveal
meanings inherent in images of action such as

the opening of before-unopened doors or the
greeting from before-unmet strangers from our own
biological chain whose humanity is as

resplendent as late afternoon light beamed onto a
lake full of pure white geese in mid-migration

Windows in the dying room are actually
also ten times larger than ones in the
living room and look out on oceans of

stars at their own height and with a
poignant intimacy in that the sight of

them shows secrets of the universe at a
glance that unfold before your eyes not only the

origin of things from His personal precincts

but also all those He has sent to tell us these things of
superb lineage and perfect equipoise before

our Compassionate Lord

such that the dying room takes precedence over the
living room in every case

as that is our most natural transposition from
one state to another and the most

natural disposition of all things watched over
continuously by the sacred vision whose
benign eyes are even occasionally
our own

7/19

THE CURE

The cure fell onto the village and everything
felt better even dying flowers in vases on windowsills
had extensions of two or three days of life

Ramps appeared to assist the ailing and
eyes appeared to watch over the sick

until voices could be heard harmonizing invisibly
with sighs of pain and discomfort

Whole hearts were made unbroken without sacrificing
the wisdom that comes from such decisive breakage

Whole families were reunited who had suspicions
one about the other until some mouths had
sealed shut against others and steely eyes had
replaced calm dispassionate eyes free of anger

Elderberry Church was cured of his constant stutter
Grandma Puffin Darlene Sotts blew her last blood clot

Hector Alizondo Plaza rose from his death bed a much
healthier color and lived for ten years more
making clocks that sang a different birdsong
every hour on the hour

Angels glided by on their sides between silver gray clouds
dispensing God's cure laterally and diagonally

until even canaries sang stronger in spite of the
confines of their life sentences in a cage

Ants worked faster and happier and even the earth itself
shone with more multicolored clays and incandescent nitrates

all because of the cry of one pure heart unbeknownst to us all
that scaled divine levels and dimensions with ease to the
starlit top of the universe in one leap without

guile asking for simple
surcease from sorrow
and release from the penury of earned or
unearned darkness for
those around it

so that even Cathbell Clarabell Scrogg benefited from behind her
severe back screen door and put down her shotgun
and released the downturn of her mouth from its
mortal trap and smiled for the
first time in her life since eleventh grade

when she and all the townspeople around her had
inwardly died
in desperate need of God's cure

7/20

THE OLD CRACKED BELL

The seven beautiful daughters of the
horrible old grouch from Rough Mountain
insisted that he treat them kindly to no avail
until one day they turned into butterflies and
flew out the window

Halberd the executioner's son pleaded with his
nearly faceless old dad to desist his detestable
employment at which his fathers face
disappeared one degree further (soon he wouldn't
have to wear the black hood at all) until
Halberd turned into a wooden soup ladle and
had to be hung by the chimney to stir the pot

How many years did the vile harridan's daughter
try to change the ways of her mother by burning her
books of spells and burying her feathers and carbonized daubs
until one day she became a set of combs purchased by the
local porcelain-skinned princess and worn in her loose blond hair
as she rode away on a roan horse

The twenty daughters of Sultan Abegnooth Slag
turned into fishermen on the Lake of Eventual Decrees
but when the sultan sent his archers to dispatch them once and for all
they turned into fish and swam like
silver sparkles downstream

The instances of such transformations are many and
fill more tomes than we'd care to remember

and even the evil librarian who tried to destroy them
found to his horror that his son and daughter

had turned into white doves repairing those
volumes with string and glue carefully pecked into
place with their sharp beaks

Each window of darkness soon has a curtain drawn
over it but when it's pulled aside again
the bright day illumines new trees new territories and
new replacements for the affections of those inclined to
injustice or sheer deviance from God's Way

So that the beaten dwarf whose own father never
admitted his paternity to him
as he lashed him as a renegade orphan
turned into a sleek young deer and
flew over the windowsill in a single harmonious glide
and bounded between new trees and continued across
new territories until he reached the highest hilltop to eat
lichen and baby ferns while his father lamented his evil to
such a degree he hanged himself one day with the
same whip he'd beaten his son with

and was transformed into that old cracked bell that
dangles today from the derelict house on the hill schoolboys throw
rocks at to make clang its many mournful notes
in metallic singsong over the desolate valley until they

finally die away

7/21

A LITTLE COURSE IN MIRACLES

Here's miracles! Crack open a seed
and a tree stands forth its green
afro full of birds!

Inside a waterdrop are
cracked galleons and wrecks of our history at sea!
Sailors wishing their sweethearts a last
goodbye! Drowned
families drinking tea!

Wind blows cornfields flat as ice
but the stalks are up again like
headdressed warriors in cornrows of formation!

Each sound we hear is part of the orchestra

Each bird we see has escaped from the
chorus to make loops in the air

Each secret thing in the forest is
known from the inside

Each heart of us is swimming together in the
open sea of His thought of us
swimming in the open sea of His thought

O angels gathered round! Your perfect
pleasure is distinct and well-attended!

No light clicked on or off but that
new universes arise! Full of dolphins and
foreclosures whale pods and bankruptcies
rainfall at sea and happy birthdays to you in Anatolia!

One ant walks its path with the rest of its hill

One clown stands on tiptoe and the whole crowd roars!

One megaton polyplath snorkdinger
smashes into Neptune and disappears in its gases
as we fry eggs and turn through our
orbit again unshaken as if for the
first time!

Hail to you also dear reader or listener! Your past present and
future worth its weight in divine emptiness

Only Allah only Allah only Allah

7/23

A SHORT TREATISE ON NIGHTMARES

A nightmare intrudes and concludes itself
until we wake up

Quick hold the red handle or quick take the
flaming rope that will open the hatch to
flush it definitively down!

Tall elm trees stand firm by Spanish rivers with
Arabic names distorted into modern speech

Hefty antagonists with demonic power take us
in their vice-like grip until we take refuge with
God against Satan and wake free

How many horses need be slaughtered in this
human race? It seems one is
more than enough

but another comes with even more savagely blazing eyes just a
head through our window with incendiary mane and a
tongue a thousand speaking snakes hissing to be heard
though the actual nightmare be far more
domestic and less mythic than this
more something gone terrifically wrong in our
usual day that takes on
monumental proportions with razor-sharp edges

A ghost ship's prow rips into our northern corridor

Up from the rip let a billion angels
stream to protect us

No demon lasts long but fangs sink deep
and leave gaping holes

the howling of distant dogs quickly fills with its
hoarse yabber

The moon past its full just above me now as I write

spreading its light on hill after rolling hill
of old olive trees in perfectly planted rows

in whose shadows who lurks if not

my own slobber self at the ready to

menace me?

7/24

DOGS BARK IN MONTEFRIO

Out in the night in Montefrio Spain under
ten billion or so brilliantly clear stars and almost
cartoon clear-cut constellations a single dog somewhere

is barking its heart out endlessly perhaps waking me up
or is trying to wake up its master against some
unjust encroachment or wake up its

comrades to join together one farm to another
against the common enemy visible or invisible or perhaps
just the night itself with all its vast fullness

poor individual pooch hawking and hacking its high-pitched
yelps over and over in the dark

solitary as each star above it is or maybe it's
trying to connect to those stars themselves to have them
or their God draw near and not be so

cosmically far away being a true
lover of loyalty and affection in its dog nature purity

even now as I've written this continuing its
plaintive and unanswered barks

*What in the world can irk it or inspire its
calling out so? Is the*

huge night so alien that at the very
funnelly bottom of it one rib-caged tail-wagging pointy-eared
pooch must stand on this earth and lift its
jaw-boned wolfish head and yelp for dear life?

Master of such dogs acknowledge this dog just this once
and let it sleep curled up again one ear always on
alert if necessary but its tail nearly encircling it with
Your protective Grace or are Your

stars answering in their way and is this
dog's monologue really a dialogue between dog and stars we can't
understand?

The Siamese cat on the other hand that
came with the cortijo we've rented for ten days
is calmly sleeping stretched out like a
pair of velvet gloves her back legs crossed
her queenly Siamese masked face serene

While out in this peaceful night under the Dipper Leo
The Seven Sisters Orion and all the other constellations visible on
the 25th of July 2005

that one dog out there somewhere
continues barking and barking in its doggy doggedness without

letup or noticeable reply

7/25

THE OLD ONES AND THE YOUNG ONES

The old ones are pushing huge woolen balls up a
small incline

The young ones are saddling ponies as fast as they can

The old ones are mouthing words from songs they
can't quite remember and lights go on in distant houses

The young ones are planting fireworks in the ground
then standing back and singing in unison in made-up languages

The old ones sit in a hundred chairs at once
under a million umbrellas

The young ones lift invisible things into the air
peer into them then set them down on water

The old ones laugh at things that make the young ones
stare straight ahead

The young ones laugh at things that toss little
barbed wire stars into their soup

The old ones have maps they say and descriptions

The young ones say they'll go there any way they can

The old ones have fourth-dimensional movies they'd like to
play for the young ones

from another era with a lot more dialog

The young ones are drawing lightningbolts on the
horizon with little silver pens they find
in boxes of popcorn

There are angels for both the old ones and the
young ones who dance on a mountaintop
seen differently by each one as triangular or
quadrilateral trapezoidal or peaked

But when day comes it turns out to be
simply domed and full of stars

                                                        7/26

THE SKI SLOPE INEVITABLE

The ski slope Inevitable whooshed us down to what was
certainly coming our way

Cantilevers and gears unseen come into play at such
moments to which it seems our best response is a
smile

Rapid fire characterizes these occurrences or else the
pyramids would still be under construction and the
fall of Rome would still look like
status quo

The Inevitable wedded so closely with His blessings upon us
though we may not always be aware of their
intense affection in every case especially when
things turn out disastrous or worse

Though everything really is about as inevitable as it can
be when you think about it even the fact that
pigs don't have wings and the price of eggs
fluctuates from moment to moment or the
sky is blue which it actually is not except what's
close at hand

We often get the impression that if only we weren't ourselves
in between what comes to us and what we are
things would go a lot smoother

The Inevitable would then be glorious festivalian
moments the levels of which would be
angelically attended up to the highest

and the depths of which would reflect back
up to our hearts with lake-like clarity upon whose dark
surface unrippled by anything but their own gliding motions
the Swans of Ecstatic Celebration would slide
in silent formation across and across endlessly

as pure as each day is as it inevitably unfolds
from within us

and takes us down its slopes to what

certainly comes our way

7/29

LOOK AT THE DOOR

for Abdal-Hadi and Salama Scott & Family

Look at the door that
crumbles when you open it

or the sun that beats down
when you least expect it

the road that ties itself in knots
to have you coming back
the way you came

or the night that listens to your inmost thoughts
then simply turns to daylight as if they were
just part of the normal course of things
with people moving around in it

Look at your shoes
empty one moment and filled the next
by the same feet you had asleep
scaling mountaintops under canopies of stars

No one comes this way twice

Some say no one comes this way once

The salt in the shaker got there through various
miraculous circumstances

but each grain is itself unique and will
never be repeated

We're sent out on an errand that God
wants us to fulfill even now as we
lean on one elbow or row down the Amazon in a skiff

A house on fire finally extinguishes itself and later
barely remembers it housed any inhabitants at all

The mouse in its hole lives for as much moment as
we do though its feelers twitch faster and its
nose wrinkles with delight at happy odors

If you've never been here before you take away
the reflection into your heart that could
never have happened without you

A dragonfly stopped in its flight having fallen into a pool
but later carried away by ants to be
devoured in the depths of the hill

It's as if there were a bright star for every one of us
when you look up from a remote mountaintop
and see more than you could possibly imagine

And perhaps we're on that bright star wondering
what on earth we're doing in this world at all

It's not inconceivable
the longest distance being only a breath away

when our breath is filled with God's invitation to Him
fulfilled

The night is so soft with its wind blowing up the valley
it seems we'd be able to float on it
into the Unseen

If you find me there greet me

I'll be waiting by the celestial Footstool
for the first time in true presence
having been absent to myself up to now

The door crumbles in your hand
the same way the world disappears behind you

so long as you move forward through its
parameters never losing sight of the goal

7/30
(written in the hills of Orgiva, Spain,
on my 65th birthday)

SPAT SUNFLOWER SEED SHELLS

1

Life is a gigantically huge mountain

that takes place within each moment

transparent then suddenly opaque

like breath on a mirror

bicycling past a forest that suddenly arises
as the bicyclist passes

with his fresh bread for home

then disappears behind him while he savors
the fresh wheaty aroma his digestive juices
already combining at attention
deep in his being

while the Gnostic on this mountaintop
enters the Unseen unseen then enters the Seen seen

by no one but his reverberant Lord

2

We actually live forever

but not our bodies

which drop off at some point

like sunflower seed shells

spat out by gypsies

                                                                              8/2

THE LACE OF LIGHT

As light settled over the village like fine powder or
very small spangles

salvation again occurred to the mind of Professor
Snoddin and he lifted lids off jars and looked in

and replaced books to their shelves in proper order
and spoke soothingly to both bird and cat cat and
mouse fire and water air and earth

His wife meanwhile seeing light settle down so in such
unusual patterns continued her tasks with their

usual precision and having tatted an enormous lace
cloth that nearly covered the entire floor of their house

snug against Lost Teardrop Hill she gazed at its
patterns of stars and tessellated angles and saw to her

cool amazement it was the same as the light outside which was now
falling in snowflake shapes against the sere grasses and

drought-anguished crops which responded by
actually coming back to life and regaining their

natural colors of strong green and dark tomato red
so that this year all was not lost but only

testingly detained until Grace at His own time
might fall

It's always this way for us in our impatience
knocking beakers off marble tabletops in our

hastening of the subtlest of elemental combinations in our
hopes of constantly circumventing time

But if we knew one moment of God's time we'd be
as vast as a handful of galaxies free-floating in their

vast space and in fact we do taste it directly in the
very moment we're in but as human bodies experiencing

bodily sensations we're hampered from this experience by
this or that tactility or discomfort or false impression
when scanning what in reality is a landscape of

divine proportions elongated at either end and
way far out in depth and height instead of

closed rooms with rugs on wooden flooring and
four walls with windows or happy or sad pictures and

that ceiling above us that always appears
far lower than it really is

Professor and Mrs. Snoddin have not been
forgotten however and are now standing together at their

front door watching angels playing among the
falling patterns of light on every surface and

glowing from every subsurface and even farther in until what their
wet eyes see are almost pools within deeper pools of

a phenomenal universe that is so transparent to them that
they are able to see also both forward and

backward in time to Adam the first prophet to
Muhammad the last and then the starlit streams forward from

him of the pure saints and their progeny asking blessings upon
him always and all of them singly and collectively each with their

particular revelation and path of instruction to us
which is that fine patterned light falling so always

perfectly upon us

8/3

CONTINUOUS TRAVEL

We're traveling now inside the giant fluted white skirts of a
swiftly huge man or woman on his or her way somewhere with total

leg-churning faith in the Originator of all travelers that we'll
arrive in one piece with our toothbrushes and favorite
reading matter at either our houses left behind in memory's fantasy clouds
with the front doors securely locked and the
cats looked after by the neighbor next door

or an outpost of cypress trees with beseeching boughs leafily touching
heaven and a series of mercury pools one bigger than the other
in ascending levels to a bronze-lit sky where
choruses of very strange creatures await us with little
name placards hoping to whisk us away in their
one-wheeled taxis to an otherworldly resort no one
ever wants to leave

Is this Paradise or that? Is this world real or
that? When will we know for sure?

The teaching tells us this world's a dream an illusion a
mental projection a heartbreak and a false front
although those with eyes to see see through it to the

symmetrical urns of sweet perfumes and coils of beneficent light that
surround all things and every live soul wandering here
on their strange journey from first uncertain steps even for
butterflies and egrets to those strong strides with tickets in
hand to finally the aged shadow-shuffle the sphinx

talked about so enigmatically tapping with a cane
like a one-legged tap dancer

But even when our enthusiasm for hectic travel falters
we're on our way and ready for whatever sweet or
sour circumstances surround us with their
huge picture windows and sudden exits either majestic or miniscule
into more worlds than anyone can imagine

and more extraordinarily glorious than any
traveler could possibly conceive

inside the giant white fluted skirts of light each man or
woman of us moves in

toward the last sipped drink at the extreme end of our path
that will turn us into doves and
finally into totally un-dissatisfied lovers

                                                                               8/4

THE ILLUMINATION OF FRAY LUIS DE SALAMANCA DE CRISIS Y BENDICIÓN

Fray Luis de Salamanca de Crisis y Bendición
sat in his tip-pointed tent in the blaze of the full moon

Everything was in silhouette even his thoughts and his prayers
An abandoned sheep stood in stone silence on the
sad hill of their exile

His lips moved almost imperceptibly except that a
big black fly kept menacing his tranquil concentration
an aggressive fat black fly no doubt from the desert or a
mutant perhaps from a
simpler and more sociable strain

He took up a holy book to swat it next time it
landed and suddenly it did and suddenly Fray Luis
had his chance

but while we have in full moonlight the picture of
unsuspecting fly on stone and Fray Luis with a holy book raised
in the air above it with an indescribable look on his face
what happened next is anyone's guess

for Fray Luis was now suddenly in Samarkand in costly silk
robes draped in necklaces of rubies and emeralds with
diamond rings on all his fingers

and the fly (for we must assume it is a she)
sits in front of him the most gorgeous lady any light however
faint or solar ever fell on
in a loose chiffon body veil barely covering her glistening
alabaster skin

"*Wait!*" she whispered to him throatily
"before you strike me dead hold still for a moment…
I have a request which I pray you'll fulfill for me
to the best of your ability"

Fray Luis was too stunned to speak so instead he just
nodded his turban-topped peacock-feathered head in silent
agreement

"I want you to imagine you are me for a moment O
holy man of this mountain and these many years of
fasting and fervent invocation

and then I want you to imagine you are a hundred
more of me as populous in my species as floating dust
falling through the air
and then multiply that in every direction until you've
nearly covered the earth in similar creatures all of us

fat black flies as annoying and vulgar as wild drunks
crashing a child's birthday fiesta

And you are one of them too Fray Luis de
Salamanca de Crisis y Bendición you are also

one of a multitude of vermin and your own life depends heavily
on the mercy of those greater than you that
surround you and the protective blessings
of the gracious Lord Who created you"

Fray Luis was perfectly adept at visualizing in detail both
subtle and minute vastness
after his years of concentration on the words of God and the
states and stations of previous saints' illuminations

but imagining himself (facing a sumptuous woman on a terrace of
sweetmeat trays and servants with steaming ewers in
gardens of cypresses to the sound of
fountains and distant lute music) as

so many flies that get into our honey jars and
sit on cut apples and pears to wash their feet then sink their
indiscriminate mandibles into with fly-like
concentration and relish

was somehow almost more than he could
bear but even so he managed in bright Technicolor
to do it

and at that moment he became a single solitary fat black fly in
a temple in ancient China and in chromium mall America and
on a futuristic machine somewhere in an
experimental station on Mars the Moon or Jupiter

a fly so common and low and disgusting that
even moonlight couldn't illumine the

hideous features of its insectoid fce

and then just as suddenly the vision faded and he was
alone again in stitched rags on his lone mountaintop with
holy book raised and black fly on rock both suspended in

eternity with all its endless winds and running water
and all its silvery light and clear-cut imagery so
brightly lit in its multitudinous ascending corridors flashing

and he heard the woman's distant soothing
voice in his ear and it said but one word only
but it said that word as an irrefutable command:

"*Now!*"

And the book came down hard
and the black fly fell dead at once

and the night grew dark as pitch
and his heart woke up in a flash

and the world turned slowly as usual on its axis
and the moonlight reemerged from behind a
fleecy cloud bank

and Fray Luis de Salamanca de Crisis y Bendición
gained the illumination he'd sought all these years of
deep penance and invocation

as his salt tears fell on the curled up fly-carcass

and wetted its hairy corpse all its legs some flexed some extended

and on all fly carcasses everywhere and
on his own and everyone else's frail bodily existence

its flying days over and Fray Luis de Salamanca's
saintly days just beginning from a point of absolute zero

in his tip-pointed tent on his solitary mountaintop
in the cold white blaze of the full moon

in simple and solitary
silhouette in the solitary night

                8/6

INVENTORY

In a little box the size of a small church
lie several pilgrims' feet severed from their limbs

In a little pink thimble the size of a Hindu temple
are arranged hundreds of devotees' delicate fingers still holding petals

In a little candy wrapper of rice paper the size of a Buddhist shrine
are lined up the closed eyes of thousands of the faithful
in spheres of gray ash

In a single black shoe the size of a synagogue
curl the emaciated bodies of the brutalized demanding
the brutalization of others

In a halva tin the size of a huge mosque
stand on their necks the severed heads of both their
victims and the victimizers
pretending not to know how it happened to happen

Box Thimble Candy Wrapper Black Shoe Halva Tin
grocery store of misbegotten objects in mirror image

Oh sell each one to a museum or trash collector
(whoever comes in as the highest bidder)

God's Voice is veiled in His Messengers' lips

clear to some but murky to others

But the man and woman alert as chipmunks
by the side of the road
go ask them for instructions
on how to divest the self and reinvest the soul

They know the score even though they're outwardly
nondescript and trembling

No one's safe from doctrinal mutilation long after the fact
of its first revelation

I'll sit here on a stool of melting ice cubes
until someone comes out from the shouting crowd

O Lord take me in again
to the original heartbeat!

                                                                8/7

SMUDGES

I cleaned off a mirror
and thought of my self
and how it needs cleaning

And thought of my shaykh
who seems to be a mirror
for everyone else

8/8

THIRTEEN PEACOCKS

The thirteen royal peacocks knew when to shriek and when
to parade their displayed finery in majestic beak-tight
silence past the Alhambra windows

they walking past topiaries of animals and dancers to the
rhythms of fountains rushing all day and night to their
own internal music

And somehow behind the latticed windows people move
more slowly and go from room to room through these
giant tessellated corridors and down long
languishing esplanades on their way somewhere

but by so passing and bypassing by these very
tiled walls not the destination alone is

the important thing but even out the sides of
their eyes the splendor brings on heart's peacefulness the way
say a horn-honking congested city street does not
though it's a veil over similar peacefulness for the

one who's at peace

And the thirteen peacocks strut through even
the most unlikely places

shrieking from time to time their raucous
peacock shrieks or simply silently striding

with their tails occasionally displaying those

black staring eyes in centers of bright iridescent green
that see nothing though
they strut in God's beauty

8/10

SAINTLY PLACES

We need to stand in saintly places
the way our body needs food to not topple over

We need to go there and find nearness there
even just a rude rock-strewn place where something

saintly took place or is taking place
tombs in giant sepulchers or a rude

rock-strewn place you can feel under your
feet or at the base of the heart the

non-physical saintliness of a real person in whom
God was by that person's pleasing Him pleased

and stand there in its crystal waters rushing
past our ears and bathing our limbs the way

careful mothers of all creatures bathe their young
in the same way really we need to

find and stand in saintly places in this world
or stand with saintly ones and

stand with them for a time or for all time
and once found not ever leave their sainted precincts

in time or out of time
but stand with them

in their saintly places or those
who have gone before whose places are still

palpably alive the way even other live places
are not but these places are refuges and

refueling places not known anywhere
else on earth or with any other practitioners

and to stand in the bounty of a saintly place is
indescribable but evident if not then

then now in its great effect and the continuous affect
it has on us to

stand just once or have stood for even a small time
in space

in saintly places

                                                              8/10

THE BELL UNRUNG

The bell unrung the cat unmeowed the earth unturned
Where would we go?

The door unopened the scoundrel unscoundreled
the table unspread
How would we live?

The road untaken the face unfocused the coop
unflown
Life unrecognized!

Each tick of the clock a seed that
falls from God's Table onto our tiny cloth

Each mishap downfall God's pause between breaths
or His breaths themselves His
loving concern for us

Each step forward or back disabused of our mortality
a wind that wraps us in His greater dimension

8/11

SCRATCHING SOUND

1

I heard a faint noise and it was
nothing really

Not the Apocalyptic rending of walls and
tearing of ceilings impaling of sheep and high-piled
pyres at all street intersections
and a constant wailing both low and high

but a tiny scratching sound at the back door or
window
and it might be the moon trying to get in out of
its lunacy

it might be the night itself tired of falling on
scenes of carnage and hypocrisy

A scritch-scratching like a cat in its cat box

Perhaps trying to articulate its name or even just
speak a known language for once

The earth moves imperceptibly to us although
with sextant and quadrant and quaint astrolabe we'd
be convinced of it for sure though in
earlier centuries we were the fixed pivot and all else
swirling around us

There it goes again
wanting in

If I ask it point blank it goes silent
Is your name Amber or Ambrose?

Silence

2

In the iron foundry where locomotives are forged
you have to shout louder over the din

You have to shout even louder if you
want to be heard especially well by
anyone but if you want to be heard at all
actually you have to have a robust growl of a voice

and it has to be louder than the making of the
iron horse the locomotive with the

pouring of molten iron in the red glow of the
forge by day or night and the
hellish glow of fire on the forgers' faces

Great iron wheels and the great cogs and levers of
the iron locomotive you have to

shout louder than to be heard at all

though in God's Forge where all the great

galaxies are made we must be

silent as tombs and quieter than our own

selves more silent than's ever permitted in
this world more

dumb even than a silent

tomb

more silent and even far more dumb

than a tomb

3

The sunrise takes place in the eyes of the
rising sunrise beholder

But it's 4:30 dawn and dark outside
and God's tents keep folding in the
invisible air

Fish are laughing

Fires are grinding their teeth
and the tents of God keep folding and folding

into greater rather than smaller
until they enfold us all

and there's a lone bicyclist on a distant hill
singing

And nothing but the swift dry rattley sound of his
strong wheel-spokes and the hum of his
tires on asphalt

and the swish of folding the constant folding until

everything gets folded in God's tent-folds

and distant stars are also enfolded

and now it's a quarter to five
and time for the Dawn Prayer

4

The night's grown silent again only the
stars sounding like crickets or is it the

crickets serenading the stars? Wishing they could
come down for once

but it's not their style

And what our galaxy has is style

Style in spades!

The way the ocean rolls back and takes another
run at it over and over

The way mountains sometimes have to step aside for their
molten-core brothers to spout off and change the
configuration of landscape and horizon then grow
silent again as if nothing had happened

The way great sea beasts move in pods and occasionally
and spectacularly surface and you know they've got an
amazing narrative that goes along with it and are
saddened by the language barrier that prevents us from
speaking humpback
the way they do with each other
in the depths and on the
surfaces

The way somehow the earth's wounds heal and
people dust the ashes off their heads and open up a
grocery store just this side of the rubble and tell
jokes that make us laugh and histories children have already
forgotten

Style of the earth where the little
scratching sound is life itself

speaking the pure
language of scratching!

8/13

THE SILVER BOAT

The silver boat weighs down the captain
blurry at his porthole but insisting on hegemony

Another instance in history of too much power concentrated
in too little mentality

Natives in palm trees calculating coconuts
can't shrink the distance impending their true destiny

Sometimes enslaved sometimes slave-owners
No one stays for long in the
realm of mortality

Stomps he does on silver heels stomps and flings his spyglass
the captain drags his silver boat and whistles out of harmony

When God's in charge of everything
who's to claim supremacy?

Billiards on a green felt field that never
spell out victory

completely

8/14

DEATH WITH A GREEN UMBRELLA / AN ENTERTAINMENT

Death came to the party holding a green umbrella
and chatting amiably about gardening so we'd think
it was life not death though three people unbeknownst
almost drowned in the pool that day of natural causes

(And what exactly are *unnatural* causes?
Even when it doesn't kill from within doesn't it at least proceed from
cause to effect? *But I digress*)

Death was darling that day in a big straw boater and
dark purple shades bare feet painted red
(or was it the devil himself?) and

a little well-tailored vest full of pockets crammed with
business cards but you
wouldn't want to take one just yet

Each time eye contact is made with Death someone makes a
perceptive remark or becomes one notch wiser suddenly as if
that distant experience years back on a beach in Honduras
for example suddenly fit into a perfectly
rational picture or the death of someone particularly
beloved hit the gong of a particularly low-pitched
reverberation in the heart to bring about wisdom

But Death was on a shopping spree and wasn't
satisfied that day that three got away

even though narrowly
so when we adjourned to an inner room for cocktails
I proposed a toast and everyone's glass was raised when I
delivered a half-hour encomium to all the living on
earth by very quickly
trying to name each one of them as if to account for
every last one and really hard were the
smallest children in Chinese junks docked in
Hong Kong's Kowloon Bay who'd gone to sleep way
inside under the
thatch and bamboo roof's cabins in warm
baskets of puppies

And Death was visibly annoyed and kept
trying to break in with some lame objection or other
but then I turned and asked
"Then who's your *family if we could be so enlightened to
know?*" And Death who is the one among us who
is more ancient than the stones and the
magnetic poles themselves but has no antecedents nor alas any
living progeny
had to pause and look anxiously about the room as if to
make eye contact but in reality to greedily claim
another for itself

And everyone now actually wise to Death at last
gathered around this well-tailored single-most
unhypocritical and most sincere one among us
(though we'd never admit it)

and glared right into Death's face to put it on the

spot but Death suddenly let out a high-pitched
Richard Widmark snicker and ducked

below us turned and curtsied and
disappeared leaving its bright green umbrella

leaning precariously against the grand piano
that was now playing very softly *The Belles of Saint Trinians*
but with no observable hands on the keys

8/15

ALBINO SILVER FOX

An albino silver fox took pains to put high on its
list of emphatic "don'ts"
"Don't get caught in a huntsman's crosshairs"

Then with slightly less priority
*"Don't light a match in a small canoe floating on a
sea of gasoline*

*Don't drive if an elephant sitting in your lap
obstructs your view of the road*

*Don't theorize grandly if you aren't willing to imagine
elaborately*

*Don't let everyone else persuade and guide you
if all but one have the heads of wild horses
and the one that doesn't is you"*

And with that our invisible protagonist goes
out into the world convinced he or she's
learned an adequate amount thank you

and has to douse the match she's lit
in a small canoe on a sea of gasoline
on the wetness of her tongue

and has to try to get the elephant to
sit in the back seat or better yet perhaps

himself sit on the elephant's head taller than most
everything with a clear horizon all the way to the
Taj Mahal

Then sitting under a tree planted there by Thomas Jefferson
she fails to imagine elaborately enough to include the
vagaries of human nature in her otherwise foolproof
plan though a fool's born every second

and as the wild horses gallop like the wind together almost in
lockhoof formation down the green slope of a mountain glade
he realizes that such freedom isn't won by simply
acting on every whim when the deepest part of the heart
and the soul's true nourishment's
not in it

8/16

THE RED FEZ

Something to do with a red fez

First a monkey wore it in the circus
Died
Monkey in an extravagant burial for a monkey
Circus band tuba player in gray cemetery in
fog cold day red fez passed on to son of
tiger master next seen worn by tiger master's
son on his bike through the tents dung pitch and
strike pitch and strike until he's too old for it

Follow the red fez

Dark night red fez by side of road
believe it or not a beaver finds it and
being an avid circus spectator puts it on head and
goes back among the beaver folk now their leader
wears it for a few days doing no work and sleepless
lest it fall off or get stolen which

one fine day it does fall off into the swift
downstream past little industrial towns eddying and
caught in polluted foam swirls but getting somehow
redder with each washing

"*Look it's a red fez*" pulling at her father's hand
relents (dirty soaking wet don't know where
it's been *well OK*)

She wears it it fits she wears all red for weeks
to match she's even got red hair it's really a
very red experience
puts it on her doll for the night
wakes up one midnight feverish to find doll
emitting light under that fez
Mommy! Mommy! but she doesn't see it
the whole room as if lightning's struck
brighter than a hundred suns with that red fez
triumphant

Yeas go by she's impelled forward by the
secret incident of the red fez that one night
though once on the subway she startled to see
someone else in a red fez but no
light explosion no illuminated subway car no giddiness among
the sullen passengers going home

"It would so have helped these people cheer up"
she thinks and looks out the blur for her stop
and steps out and misses seeing someone

else in a red fez shoot down a corridor
hers is at home in a drawer in a little
black velvet bag back behind the underwear

I'm not sure if this needs to conclude or
go anywhere it's a red fez tale worth its
weight in red felt

That's all though I think it tells something about

inner readiness because she becomes a
scholar with an uncanny way of elucidating
meanings that often surprise her
saying things out of her mouth she's never
thought but which have a reddish glow to them
and impart to others the sensation of
wearing a jaunty but noble red fez

Some inventors a few physicists one veterinarian and
a successful crooner had the red fez experience as
her students

And one night late in a diner the crooner's serenading an old
couple on their fiftieth and the old man
dies in the booth holding his dear wife's

hand and they bury him but when they
pass by his coffin *behold!*

He's wearing a red fez

8/20

PRUNING

I wonder if the young sugar maple tree I planted from a
tiny sapling a couple of years ago

appreciated that my pruning it yesterday was for its
own good

giving it shape and longevity since some
gardening advisors have said to

cut it down and plant a fancier ornamental of some
kind even a flowering dogwood or something with

pale pink blossoms but I've resisted

and now it's a thin teenager getting tallish and
in the words of one friend *"gawky"* with some

sparse spots along its trunk where no branches are which is
why he suggested some pruning here and there to

encourage growth along shapelier lines
and of course I may be exaggerating when I say that I

seemed to hear it cry out in shock and pain as I
cut into a few of its heftier but over-extended branches

and thought of *"The Secret Life of Plants"* those touching but
slightly dubious scientific experiments of a

decade or so ago that proved plants have feelings which I
actually do not doubt as everything else seems to too

including perhaps in a somberer way rocks and dirt
clods and sea-waves

And wonder also if a pirate thinks it's pruning when his
leg's cut off and replaced with a wooden peg

or someone blinded after seeing can think of the growth
opportunity in literally unforeseen directions in a world

transformed into a non-visual dimension

Those loppings and sudden slicings we might encounter
completely unprepared in our lives for

anything but wild growth and continued unlimited
expansion forever

though my teenage friend here fits so much better into the
corner of the garden with a few deft branches now

hovering lightly over the classical birdbath
in our very small but somehow elegant

row house and recently patio'd backyard where angels the size of
Mount Vesuvius could just as easily fit and feel

right at home

8/24

ONE TOTALLY TALL TALE

By all standards of compression I should be
able to write a single line that accordians

out to tell one totally tall tale so full of
detail you'd think it's the city

under the El in its vernacular contradictions
contractions and contraptions

light and darkness and the constant flicker between them
of Tahitian isles with mango skies and papaya shores

no need for decorum all on a sliver of silver

worn around the neck of an adventurer or mountain climber
who's about to ascend into high Arctic regions

and lose the power of speech altogether
in exchange for visions of ecstatically dancing

spirits and sylphs who live in icier domains
and keep warm enough for life by singing like

aurora borealises in shifting curtains of close harmonies
color mostly cobalt and lavender red and pale purple

But these lines aren't quite the story I should be
able to tell rather the story of molecular

terrestrial and extraterrestrial realities that God
sets into motion by the softest of outbreaths

under the allegiance of His Bountiful Gaze
with all His Speech pouring through us

and all our eyesight or lack thereof also
His own and the sanctified view of what He Sees

through our eyes but without the distractions of
form rather the endlessly fountaining out from the

wells of meaning into some fleeting shape or other then
dissolving back into formlessness again

so fast our own creations and constant recreations can't quite
focus on it as our own disintegrations and reconstitutions

take place under an endlessly blue sky as
yellow as the petals of sunflowers in

further evidence of His breezes and sweetly
unsinister decrees

8/28

THE SEVEN DWARVES

I love it when my wife comes downstairs to my
studio and falls asleep on my couch

She's my own private Princess
and I'm her Seven Dwarves

gazing on her beauty

8/28

ALL FROM A DOT

The silent dot sandwiched between a humming supernova and
the thunderous popping-into-place of a Black Hole

is the diacritical speck under the *"ba"* in the *bismillah*
In The Name of Allah Most Merciful Most Clement

of a new creation
all of us packed tighter than tight in a
little black dot in space out from whose

intense confines will grow (when it's of
substantial planetoidal mass)

swaying palm trees and perfect rows of olives
and us perhaps (should He be so kind)

as He's said He can roll up creation and
create it anew it's not a problem for Him

so that vibrating silver streamlined emblem in space you see
isn't that but actual creation coming into focus the swiftest of

ways each thing as if with wings and a
jet propelled motor moving it colossally

forward and outward from a darkness so dense nothing
can be said to breathe there

so curled into itself like miles of seminal vesicles
and so philosophically dense as well as to not be a

movement of mind exactly but as it expands into
perceptual view it resembles a horizon all

bronze with sunrise as if a series of black lakes
spread out before a dawning sky which has

also come into being recently component of the
earthly and dragon-like creative energies of

whatever magnetically stands with fire in its belly
down below

and takes a bow and is
grateful for another opportunity

to rise

dew drops brushing away from the

smile on its face

and huge gray elephants beginning to move through the
misty grass in their daily vegetarian devouring

campaign to feed their
insatiable bulks

8/30

THE IMAM OF OUR MOSQUE

The imam of our mosque has the curious habit
of arriving on horseback

except that he hasn't got a horse so he makes those
Monty Python clippity-clop sounds with his tongue
and insists on dismounting just outside the

mosque door giving the invisible reins to one of the
kufi'd and robed boys to look after during his
Khutba

It wouldn't be so bad if it didn't neigh very loudly
during the first half and make that

blubbery mouth sound during the second

One Friday he came as a goldfish in a bowl
and gave his sermon from the steps of the *mimbar* with the

microphone right up against the glass
which was all right until it came

time to do the prayer and we couldn't tell
when he was in *sajda*

One Friday he came as a swarm of bees through the
side window and swarmed onto the wooden sides of the

mimbar so loudly we could hardly hear his words
for the magnificence of his buzzing

Once he came as a penguin
and the Mosque Committee welcomed him all

dressed in their tuxes with their
hands behind their backs and their ties askew

and he managed to weave into his sermon
various exotic Antarctic experiences and the long hours spent

incubating his wife's egg under his feet

A trapeze artist a vase of flowers a
sea wave sloshing back and forth in a tank

even once as a minor earthquake and then
with his spectacles tilted on his nose and the shakes of the
aftershocks evident in his twitches he told of the

mysteries at the center of the earth to which we are
normally not privy except through his kind mouthpiece

Next week he's coming as the Spiral Galaxy
which should be illuminating and we've

vacuumed and painted the walls so the increased
light given off by its sun and planets won't show the bad

stains and cracks that have come from our

sins supplications and above all negligence

And when he comes next month as the cries of a distant shepherd
calling his sheep I hope we'll behave

well enough to benefit from his care and his crook
to not wander as wantonly over the pastures and hills

but arrive safely under God's
bright blue sky in the open air

8/31

MY USUAL AIRPLANE APPREHENSIONS

1

I'm not fond of flying in airplanes
but I'm also not fond of Russian Roulette

though I've survived so far each time
I've flown

2

A man in blue baseball cap in a seat
in front of me is reading a paperback entitled
"Wild Stories" but I can't read the author's
name or what in fact the stories are about

Moose and muskrats? Gypsies with knives in
Spanish barrios? People suddenly throwing aside all
scruples and dancing on tables or running nude through
stadiums? Or suddenly letting the

dark forests of deeper selves fan out to their
surfaces until their eyes glisten and their
tongues become as truly eloquent as their

just as suddenly more graceful gestures and
thoughts? That seeming
"wildness" most of us repress which is
more true to our intrinsic nature such as

carrying a tray full of flowers through a
bamboo grove or

standing as still as possible in an onrushing crowd
to collect not only our thoughts but also

the gleam of stars and the stirring of
planets though unseen and unfelt directly

yet sweetly influential in our being planetary
creatures on earth

with divine starlight coursing through our
veins

3

There's a man in my row doing a crossword
with a pen —

Now I know we'll land safely!

9/5

WHILE WAITING TO APPEAR IN TRAFFIC COURT

Inside the choppy sea a tunnel of light opens up
in the heart of the person lost in it

Somewhere far off suddenly becomes everywhere up close
even the wheeling birds in silhouette against the sun

A dark hand doesn't completely come down over the night
and the white dress at the window is clothing a body of smoke

The sound of motors the sound of throbbing engines the roar of lions
don't completely drown out a single cricket's chirp

If we draw lines between all the stars as we gaze at them from below
will we have woven a tight-fitting cap for our spacious heads?

A tiny sponge moves that much closer to her mother
a bit of planetary debris in a neighboring galaxy falls

into its solar center

The lost one at sea either is lost or enters a state of pure lostness
in which like earth in its elliptical orbit is concentrically found

and the metrical gauge for all this is always spinning round

9/7

CONVERSING BEYOND THE END OF TIME

Conversations are endless

An owl conversing with its alertness
head swiveling wide eyes like laser planets

A road conversing with all the wheels that
roll over it

A rabbit conversing among cabbages in a huddle so as
to be unseen by anyone taller

Rails of light that spray upward in all
directions keeping everything on track

These backs and forths that are constant in their
inelegant or elegant chatter as if
placidly over tea or at the edge of an entertaining
cliff that sinks sheer away to cattle-filled valleys below

their hooves conversing with both marsh and earth clumps as they
moo along munching and conversing with their slow bovine dreams

And then there are the between-worlds conversations
from the unseen dimensions to the seen
whose replies may go unarticulated but whose sweet
arguments are heard ubiquitously around the world
in sleep or awake

Chitter of sea-surface microbial insectivores or
elephant-sized unknown denizens of the deeps we haven't yet
discovered conversing quite naturally with both
their big spouses and antiquity

Light actually flooding the entire world with its
crisp vocabulary of each thing carefully outlined and
presented with always its best foot forward and face shining
while the gossip goes on between sound and the
air it floats through air and the vacuum it
fills with its deep contemplative ruminations

And the wonderful conversation at all times
day and night between nothingness and this

splendidly grammatical reality we verbalize through as if there
were no punctuation until the

end as we see it and even

then it's a run-on sentence into sweet oblivion's
non-oblivious dimension of our first

face to face conversation with God in which
our transparency shows through as it
always has to

He in His ceaselessly multiplied conversational monologue
with each one of us

beyond the end of time

THE BALLAD OF THE TYRANT

The tyranny of Boulderoak the knavery of Dor
the flat out death at Zonderzee
the corpses on the floor

The scepter of the ruler in a leaden box of fire
you can't describe the way the people
listen to the liar

If one soul shouts they all shout if one soul yells they yell
but if one were suddenly to sing
they'd send that soul to Hell

The air is fogged with extra noise the ears are clogged with ice
I can't imagine what their hearts are like
but bungalows for mice

If one tells truth here eyes go wild arms wave feet kick
that person might as well be stoned
death less painful less thick

The one-eyed man is king here except he's put to death
the tyrant can't let anyone who sees
even take a breath

The night falls they're all eyeless voiceless heartless cold
the gold chair the tyrant sits on
keeps their poor souls sold

Kill the tyrant hang him by his feet or rip his head off
he'd stand back up and grow it back
and be like Boris Karloff

The people make the tyrant bold the people keep him strong
until they change he'll keep them down
and bang them like a gong

9/10

THE USUAL CLOCKS TICKING

The domes glittered in the far twilight as
light and dark don't obey the laws of

far or near but are always close up to us like a
second skin

And imagine our existence without either as if
dark and light could be lifted away for once and

we'd be in a huge windy warehouse on the
edge of some desert perhaps with only the low

grumble of dissatisfied camels and the wind

but such would be impossible as light is like
an extension of our souls and really so is

darkness O beware my soul to let only
light be your soul mate!

But as I said the domes glittered in the
far twilight for whatever reason it needs to be

far rather than near the turquoise tiles catching
just one quick light slap of light before the

sun slides down and out of sight
and a brash efflorescence of crows blows across the

sky at that moment and the last donkey rider passes by
with sacks of flour and rice on either side a

youth really of only twelve with more than twenty
years inside him already and the donkey about

ready to die altogether which it will do
peacefully after eating its fill in twelve

days and eleven more trips just like this one and the
boy will grieve as his donkey's his oldest

friend and though smelly and obdurate really his
only relative though of a distant species since

our anonymous donkey driver was orphaned early and
brought up by surly neighbors but right now let's

concentrate on the picturesque scene before us of
dome catching light and a lazy silhouette below it of

donkey and sacks and youth going past and
a flock of crows blowing upward like a graceful fan across the

sky's remaining light and a sea breeze and the
soft tinkling of glass chimes somewhere not actually in this

picture but behind me in the room where I'm
writing this at 5:45 A.M. and there's only the

usual whispering of sound and the usual clocks ticking

9/13

DEAR EYES

Dear eyes God's coefficients I can

feel the two of you up on the sides of my
face
not opposed like birds' eyes or dolphins' but

the pair of you like sentinels or lanterns at
port and starboard of a boat as it
cuts its smooth or choppy way through
easy or high seas closed or open estuaries

O eyes you two-way orbs you globes rolling
not far in one direction or the other yet
cast a glance yonder over Arizona buttes and you
get nearby to a baby-blue heaven or squint at the needle used to
thread one yarn end through the needle's eye so
elusively eye to eye that no rich man nor
camel can get through

A field of wild horses running full tilt
or an almond fallen onto a carpet blending almost
successfully in except that

you two O eyes can usually spot the
little red brown lump out of the flat carpet nap
and I can then pop its hard sweetness into my mouth-maw
equally invisible under you to me but once open
a veritable thoroughfare for good or ill also

both ways if I don't remain vigilant

O eyes you're a street full of slick prostitutes in black vinyl
tighter than penguins

or the blazing loftiness of fleecy silver clouds thousands of
angelic feet in the air during plane flights

You both judicially neutral windows painting
inside my Sistine indelible sights

I pray for your safety now and your longevity
to let light in and something of my heart out to others
for years to come
until I see the auras around things blow out like
solar flares to encompass all things in

God's holy effulgence from this single stereoscopic nearsighted
point past matter's seven seas and lush tropical paradises

and the soul see without your mistable portals
things of Light directly and your own two
optical workaholics let rest at last in the

soft velvets of their dark having seen
all the worlds they can see in as

many blinks it takes them like ticking clocks to see
there in my head where I feel you now

as my lids close over you in momentary sleep

9/18

IT'S TRUE

1

I stood at the door of a strangely skeletal convent
where crickets wore the habits of nuns
and called for a cup of steam and distant
whistling

Shuffling accompanied a displacement of the air
and curtains flew up at the bias as if
creatures of light were wrapping themselves up in their
folds

Then it all stopped and I saw I was writing this
poem with the back screen door open onto the
too warm Philadelphia night with wars and raging
floods in September of 2005 and the

crickets sound in the dark as if they're
rattling key chains or sawing wood with their
legs

2

The law broke down at just the point when
delicate balance was needed

and moths took advantage of the lapse to burst

out of their little cotton-sock sleeping bags they'd so carefully
placed in the crook of a tree or rib of patio umbrella

and filled the air with soundless jubilation which in most
ways compensated for the void and even filled the
need for coordinated and systematically graceful
behavior that followed an innate structure so
ancient we're still finding fossils that speak in detail the
tables of the legal record

Except of course for flying horses and people who
walk on their heads

They're conspicuously absent

3

It's true that topazes litter the ground

It's true that angels walk around in normal clothes

It's true that wheels rotate to the point of invisibility

It's true that whatever beauty we saw before
is augmented into living alabaster perfection

It's true the air is waves of music

It's true that eyes tell stories mouths are dumb
to articulate

It's true that water slides without gravity through
channels in the air

and the air is prismatic gazelle-like leapings into
splintered curtains of light that open to reveal

what the mind longs for but is unable to
conceive in its purest lineaments

what the heart sees directly without
glass stairways or material representation

that nothing has passed or will pass but the
passing instant each time

and it's true that time is a pearl
dewdrop at the lip edge of a silver petal that

hovers over Paradise

9/20

"SPARE PARTS SPARE PARTS!"

"Spare parts! Spare Parts!" said the bicyclist as he
pedaled by

somewhere here in the shadow of the tallest
mountain in the world under a

sky that's definitely got it in for us so
squally and ferocious

But the spare parts man is now fitting one of our
children with a new head so often did we

hear her complain of her no-good cranial drawer and
all its contents but we cautioned her

here in the shadow of God's personal peak
that removal and substitution for what God had

spun out of divine nothingness in the first place with its
trembling lower lip and its cute dimple

might bring about unforeseen results she'd
live to regret why not a new arm say or a new foot

with freshly unpainted toenails?

But she heeded not and now has the face of a
drunken wrestler glowering under a

wrestling ring spotlight and I wonder really what its
owner looks like now and I doubt what's inside this one's

drawer is any improvement over the last
which at least didn't give us such a

fright at breakfast with her look so perpetually
and aggressively of someone about to throw one of us

through a wall for really
no reason at all

9/23

CONVERSATIONS OVER THE GRAVEYARD

Conversations arose over the graveyard
without any need for exterior reception devices

like audible thought balloons with some thoughts
more distinct than others or more terrible

words tumbling upwards like bubbles on updrafts
shining almost phosphorescent greenish-white in the full moonlight

with an economy of words but a surfeit of feeling
as if last thoughts of people sinking in quicksand who

know they're sinking so they don't so much
panic as pour words out in a rush in the possibly vain

hope that they'll finish their thoughts from
absolute A to Z before fading completely

under the ground so although these good people were
all of them literally "underground" at this point

still their hush-hush-now-don't-go-telling-anybody-this-is
just-between-you-and-me conversations almost

danced in the night air above where their bones or
saintly bodies lay (saints never decomposing)

and the babies were mature beyond their years and
the mothers dead in childbirth were full of motherly feelings

and the criminals were busy explaining themselves as if to
absolve themselves of any guilt beyond their circumstances

and the suicides were in a serious pickle having
wrenched control of the divine steering wheel of their lives

momentarily out of God's Hands as it were
and now kept heading for the same cliff or glacier

over and over yet they too no longer unable to
resist the undertow of their misfortunes

and the nurse kept waiting to comfort the others
and the magistrate kept going over the cases of those

nearest and the lovers entangled in fate's interruptions
voiced in a lyrical way surprise and death's characteristic longing for

what lies beyond eye heart and head's ability to
see yet all of them were as if whispering in an outside

corridor of heaven before gaining admittance
and all of them exhibited the unrestrained

poignancy of the human predicament easily
audible above ground in life if we only

listen more closely as God has directed both
speaker and hearer in every case as if the

deepest cello inside all of us were being

played by a serious maestro and the

deepest drum were being beaten actually by
God Himself in the guise of the human heartbeat

9/25

THE LAST POEM

It came to me after prayer this morning the
inconceivability of the last of anything as if

after it we'd hit a brick wall

The last breath the last thought the last
prayer after which all is still and silent

absolute zero absolute *"the game is up"* the
last waltz ¾'d into 0/0 with no fancy steps afterwards

and no walking away to join another circus
the last trapeze the last look at the lion
right in the face that utterly alien stare

the last applause all hands frozen in space

last sight of colored lights across a canyon in
striated streamers with wheeling birds

last words on bated last breath or last
word or last vowel last consonant last
gasp

How really in the lovely flow of things right
now from day to day even with its

majestic sameness it's inconceivable to me any
actual lastness the numbers of these so

cherished things ticking away in diminished digits
like a taxi meter going in reverse from a

set but seeming to us infinite number as it's
just as inconceivable that we start at birth with a

set number of breaths and heartbeats as if on a
big celestial board to the exact integer and each

breath and heartbeat we use up knocks one whole
integral number

down

                                                        10/4

THE BROTHER TO THE DOG

The brother to the dog who ate the newspaper was
also the father of the dog who trekked through
five states to reach home on its own
and whose great grandfather sniffed contraband on
New York's pier when the

Excelsis drew near the wharf filled with
opium and ripped the pilings and three men drowned
on a disaster Tuesday long forgotten except by the

longshoreman's great grandchildren who have
problems of their own

And angels rise in continuous sheets not only
behind all these scenes but also
straight up through their centers

to a music barely caught by strings or tiny pianos or bells
and yet the dogs in this piece however doggedly
doggy they are chasing squirrels and other dogs

know the music in their inner ear and you can see them almost
enviously following the upward arc of angels

from time to time
with their dark wet eyes

10/6

THE FIRE BROKE OUT

1

The fire broke out in a walnut shell the
size of a tiny boat crossing the Atlantic

and the resulting conflagration lit up all our
faces as if we'd been facing the resonance of a

bronze gong in the Imperial Palace so

utterly golden our expressions as we peered over the
edge at the distantly rolling green valley leading our eyes

willingly to the farthest horizon now the perfect stage for a
perfect sunrise after the

world's ashy obliteration each ash-flake

falling perfectly into the palms of our

hands just big enough for a walnut shell to fit
snugly in potential conflagration

2

The fire burst through the window but the
window was already gone

It burst through the "wind" of the window but the
wind too was gone

Now it had only a tiny "ow" to burst through and it
had better burst quick or else it would have just a

"w" to burst through and the jaggedy peaks of the "w" aren't
much though fire doesn't need much to blaze into a

giant conflagration flaming the planet whole from
equator to equator and from pole to pole like those

other blazing orbs in space that become suns

3

The same fire that licks the base of the Parthenon
licks us all

*What a sweet tongue for a fire! What
girls in shell boats ride its waves!*

How can it reduce us all to shadows
and every mountain in the world as well

so that the indestructible souls of us all are set free?

This is not a burning fire but a light
whose instantaneous slow conflagration illuminates all

the way it must be seen in eternal
flickerings

ourselves as we leave us and enter us
leaving our doors ajar for a more

splendid radiance

as endlessly present as was its presence without
discernible origination suddenly among us

lighting up the world

10/12-24

INDEX

A Little Course in Miracles   53
A Short Treatise on Nightmares   55
Afloat Behind the Face of Things   42
Albino Silver Fox   95
All From a Dot   105
Amethyst Thimble   30
British Air Flight 68 to Heathrow   40
Continuous Travel   71
Conversations Over the Graveyard   126
Conversing Beyond the End of Time   113
Dear Eyes   119
Death With a Green Umbrella / An Entertainment   92
Dogs Bark in Montefrio   57
Dream-Words upon Waking   23
Harbingers of Death   27
Inventory   78
It's True   121
Look at the Door   63
Lost Identity   24
My Usual Airplane Apprehensions   110
One Totally Tall Tale   102
Orangutan or Pit   36
Perfect World   41
Pruning   100
Saintly Places   83
Scratching Sound   86
Smudges   80
Somewhere in the Remote Arctic   39
"Spare Parts Spare Parts!"   124
Spat Sunflower Seed Shells   66
The Ballad of the Tyrant   115

The Bell Unrung   85
The Brother to the Dog   131
The Cure   49
The Dead Pirate's One Last Swing   14
The Delirious Archer   11
The Dying Room   46
The Fire Broke Out   132
The Hearts of the Holiest   44
The High Potency of Certain Moments   38
The Illumination of Fray Luis De Salamanca de
    Crisis y Bendición   73
The Imam of Our Mosque   107
The Lace of Light   68
The Last Poem   129
The Old Cracked Bell   51
The Old Ones and the Young Ones   59
The Red Fez   97
The Secret of Poetry   16
The Seven Dwarves   104
The Silver Boat   91
The Ski Slope Inevitable   61
The Star Catcher   12
The Usual Clocks Ticking   117
Thirteen Peacocks   81
Travel Notes   32
While Waiting to Appear in Traffic Court   112
Words and Birdsong   19
Words for a Preface by Tom Clark   8
Zero   21

ABOUT THE AUTHOR

Born in 1940 in Oakland, California, Daniel Abdal-Hayy Moore had his first book of poems, *Dawn Visions*, published by Lawrence Ferlinghetti of City Lights Books, San Francisco, in 1964, and the second in 1972, *Burnt Heart/Ode to the War Dead*. He created and directed *The Floating Lotus Magic Opera Company* in Berkeley, California in the late 60s, and presented two major productions, *The Walls Are Running Blood*, and *Bliss Apocalypse*. He became a Sufi Muslim in 1970, performed the Hajj in 1972, and lived and traveled throughout Morocco, Spain, Algeria and Nigeria, landing in California and publishing *The Desert is the Only Way Out*, and *Chronicles of Akhira* in the early 80s (Zilzal Press). Residing in Philadelphia since 1990, in 1996 he published *The Ramadan Sonnets* (Jusoor/City Lights), and in 2002, *The Blind Beekeeper* (Jusoor/Syracuse University Press). He has been the major editor for a number of works, including *The Burdah* of Shaykh Busiri, translated by Hamza Yusuf, and the poetry of Palestinian poet, Mahmoud Darwish, translated by Munir Akash. He is also widely published on the worldwide web: *The American Muslim, DeenPort*, and his own website and poetry blog, among others: *www.danielmoorepoetry.com, www.ecstaticxchange.com*. He has been poetry editor for *Seasons Journal, Islamica Magazine,* a 2010 translation by Munir Akash of *State of Siege*, by Mahmoud Darwish (Syracuse University Press), and *The Prayer of the Oppressed*, by Imam Muhammad Nasir al-Dar'i, translated by Hamza Yusuf. In 2011, 2012 and 2014 he was a winner of the Nazim Hikmet Prize for Poetry. In 2013 he won an American Book Award, and in 2013 and 2014 was listed among The 500 Most Influential Muslims for his poetry. *The Ecstatic Exchange Series* is bringing out the extensive body of his works of poetry (a complete list of published works on page 2).

POETIC WORKS by Daniel Abdal-Hayy Moore
Published and Unpublished

Dawn Visions (published by City Lights, 1964)
Burnt Heart/Ode to the War Dead (published by City Lights, 1972)
This Body of Black Light Gone Through the Diamond (printed by Fred Stone, Cambridge, Mass, 1965)
On The Streets at Night Alone (1965?)
All Hail the Surgical Lamp (1967)
States of Amazement (1970)

Abdallah Jones and the Disappearing-Dust Caper (published by The Ecstatic Exchange/Crescent Series, 2006)
'Ala ud-Deen and the Magic Lamp (published by The Ecstatic Exchange, 2011)
The Chronicles of Akhira (1981) (published by Zilzal Press with Typoglyphs by Karl Kempton, 1986; published in Sparrow on the Prophet's Tomb by The Ecstatic Exchange, 2009)
Mouloud (1984) (A Zilzal Press chapbook, 1995; published in Sparrow on the Prophet's Tomb by The Ecstatic Exchange, 2009)
The Crown of Creation (1984) (published by The Ecstatic Exchange, 2012)
The Look of the Lion (The Parabolas of Sight) (1984)
The Desert is the Only Way Out (completed 4/21/84) (Zilzal Press chapbook, 1985)
Atomic Dance (1984) (am here books, 1988)
Outlandish Tales (1984)
Awake as Never Before (12/26/84) (Zilzal Press chapbook, 1993)
Glorious Intervals (1/1/85) (Zilzal Press chapbook, ?)
Long Days on Earth/Book I (1/28 – 8/30/85)
Long Days on Earth/Book II (Hayy Ibn Yaqzan)
Long Days on Earth/Book III (1/22/86)
Long Days on Earth/Book IV (1986)
The Ramadan Sonnets (Long Days on Earth/Book V) (5/9 – 6/11/86) (published by Jusoor/City Lights Books, 1996) (republished as Ramadan Sonnets by The Ecstatic Exchange, 2005)
Long Days on Earth/Book VI (6-8/30/86)
Holograms (9/4/86 – 3/26/87)
History of the World (The Epic of Man's Survival) (4/7 – 6/18/87)
Exploratory Odes (6/25 – 10/18/87)

The Man at the End of the World (11/11 – 12/10/87)
The Perfect Orchestra (3/30 – 7/25/88)(published by The Ecstatic Exchange, 2009)
Fed from Underground Springs (7/30 – 11/23/88)
Ideas of the Heart (11/27/88 – 5/5/89)
New Poems (scattered poems, out of series, from 3/24 – 8/9/89)
Facing Mecca (5/16 – 11/11/89) (published by The Ecstatic Exchange, 2014)
A Maddening Disregard for the Passage of Time (11/17/89 – 5/20/90) (published by The Ecstatic Exchange, 2009)
The Heart Falls in Love with Visions of Perfection (6/15/90 – 6/2/91)
Like When You Wave at a Train and the Train Hoots Back at You (Farid's Book) (6/11 – 7/26/91) (published by The Ecstatic Exchange, 2008)
Orpheus Meets Morpheus (8/1/91– 3/14/92)
The Puzzle (3/21/92 – 8/17/93)(published by The Ecstatic Exchange, 2011)
The Greater Vehicle (10/17/93 – 4/30/94)
A Hundred Little 3-D Pictures (5/14/94 – 9/11/95) (published by The Estatic Exchange, 2013)
The Angel Broadcast (9/29 – 12/17/95)
Mecca/Medina Time-Warp (12/19/95 – 1/6/96) (published as a Zilzal Press chapbook, 1996)(published in Sparrow on the Prophet's Tomb, 2009)
Miracle Songs for the Millennium (1/20 – 10/16/96)(published by The Ecstatic Exchange, 2014)
The Blind Beekeeper (11/15/96 – 5/30/97) (published 2002 by Jusoor/Syracuse University Press)
Chants for the Beauty Feast (6/3 – 10/28/97)(published by The Ecstatic Exchange, 2011
You Open a Door and it's a Starry Night (10/29/97 – 5/23/98) (published by The Ecstatic Exchange, 2009)
Salt Prayers (5/29 – 10/24/98) (published by The Ecstatic Exchange, 2005)
Some (10/25/98 – 4/25/99) (published by The Ecstatic Exchange, 2014)
Flight to Egypt (5/1 – 5/16/99)
I Imagine a Lion (5/21 – 11/15/99) (published by The Ecstatic Exchange, 2006)
Millennial Prognostications (11/25/99 – 2/2/2000) (published by the Ecstatic Exchange, 2009)
Shaking the Quicksilver Pool (2/4 – 10/8/2000) (published by The Ecstatic Exchange, 2009)
Blood Songs (10/9/2000 – 4/3/2001)(Published by The Ecstatic Exchange, 2012)

The Music Space (4/10 – 9/16/2001) (published by The Ecstatic Exchange, 2007)

Where Death Goes (9/20/2001 – 5/1/2002) (published by The Ecstatic Exchange, 2009)

The Flame of Transformation Turns to Light (99 Ghazals Written in English) (5/14 – 8/21/2002) (published by The Ecstatic Exchange, 2007)

Through Rose-Colored Glasses (7/22/2002 – 1/15/2003) (published by The Ecstatic Exchange, 2007)

Psalms for the Broken-Hearted (1/22 – 5/25/2003) (published by The Ecstatic Exchange, 2006)

Hoopoe's Argument (5/27 – 9/18/03)

Love is a Letter Burning in a High Wind (9/21 – 11/6/2003) (published by The Ecstatic Exchange, 2006)

Laughing Buddha/Weeping Sufi (11/7/2003 – 1/10/2004) (published by The Ecstatic Exchange, 2005)

Mars and Beyond (1/20 – 3/29/2004) (published by The Ecstatic Exchange, 2005)

Underwater Galaxies (4/5 – 7/21/2004) (published by The Ecstatic Exchange, 2007)

Cooked Oranges (7/23/2004 – 1/24/2005 (published by The Ecstatic Exchange, 2007)

Holiday from the Perfect Crime (1/25 – 6/11/2005) (published by The Ecstatic Exchange, 2011)

Stories Too Fiery to Sing Too Watery to Whisper (6/13 – 10/24/2005) (published by The Ecstatic Exchange, 2014)

Coattails of the Saint (10/26/2005 – 5/10/2006) (published by The Ecstatic Exchange, 2006)

In the Realm of Neither (5/14/2006 – 11/12/06) (published by The Ecstatic Exchange, 2008)

Invention of the Wheel (11/13/06 – 6/10/07)(published by The Ecstatic Exchange, 2010)

The Sound of Geese Over the House (6/15 – 11/4/07)

The Fire Eater's Lunchbreak (11/11/07 – 5/19/2008) (published by The Ecstatic Exchange, 2008)

Sparks Off the Main Strike (5/24/2008 – 1/10/2009)(published by The Ecstatic Exchange, 2010)

Stretched Out on Amethysts (1/13 – 9/17/2009)(published by The Ecstatic Exchange, 2010)

The Throne Perpendicular to All that is Horizontal (9/18/09 – 1/25/10) (published by The Ecstatic Exchange, 2014)

In Constant Incandescence (2/10 – 8/13/10) (published by The Ecstatic Exchange, 2011)

The Caged Bear Spies the Angel (8/30/10 – 3/6/11)(published by The Ecstatic Exchange, 2010)

This Light Slants Upward (3/7 – 10/13/11)

Ramadan is Burnished Sunlight (part of This Light Slants Upward, published separately by The Ecstatic Exchange, 2011)

The Match That Becomes a Conflagration (10/14/11 – 5/9/12)

Down at the Deep End (5/10 – 8/3/12) (published by The Ecstatic Exchange, 2012)

Next Life (8/9/12 – 2/12/13) (published by The Ecstatic Exchange, 2013)

The Soul's Home (2/13 – 10/8/13) (published by The Ecstatic Exchange, 2014)

Eternity Shimmers & Time Holds its Breath (10/10/13 – 1/27/14) (published by The Ecstatic Exchange, 2014)

He Comes Running (part of Eternity Shimmers, published as an Ecstatic Exchange Chapbook, 2014)

The Sweet Enigma of it All (1/29 – 6/18/14)

Let Me See Diamonds Everywhere I Look (6/18/14 –)

www.ingramcontent.com/pod-product-compliance
Lightning Source LLC
Chambersburg PA
CBHW020909090426
42736CB00008B/543